Liberty, Equality, Sisterhood

Liberty, Equality, Sisterhood

On the Emancipation of Women in Church and Society

by ELISABETH MOLTMANN-WENDEL

translated from the German
by Ruth Gritsch

FORTRESS PRESS   Philadelphia

Library of Congress Cataloging in Publication Data

Moltmann-Wendel, Elisabeth.
  Liberty, equality, sisterhood.

  Translation of Freiheit, Gleichheit, Schwesterlichkeit.
  Bibliography: p.
  1. Feminism. 2. Women and Religion. I. Title.
HQ1154.M64513   301.41′2   77-15240
ISBN 0-8006-1325-2

6503A78   Printed in the United States of America   1-1325

Contents

Preface   7

Women in the New Testament   9
  Introduction   9
  The Gospel's Irruption into the Ancient World   12
  The New Testament   26

Four Stations on the Road to Woman's Coming of Age   41
  I. Intellectual-Political Coming of Age   41
  II. Economic Coming of Age   47
  III. Social Coming of Age   54
  IV. The Body's Coming of Age   62

Woman between Self-Surrender and Self-Assertion   69

Theses Regarding the Emancipation of Women
  in Church and Society   89

Bibliography   93
  Women in the New Testament   93
  Four Stations on the Road to Woman's
    Coming of Age   94

Preface

These essays are based on lectures I have given during the past two years at women's conferences. The women themselves chose the topics, which therefore mirror questions and wishes regarding woman's position in church and society. Other women's groups took up these topics, and the present form of these essays is a result of discussions and suggestions made in these groups. I have been asked repeatedly to publish the lectures, since there is still very little literature available on this subject. So this volume is addressed primarily to those women who, on the road to self-discovery, have found little significant support from theologians.

The very active feminist and Socialist women's groups in Germany still believe the opinions of their ideological mentors, Simone de Beauvoir and August Bebel, to be valid: that Christianity contributed essentially to the subjugation of woman. Our churches' nervous and defensive stance in regard to the question of women's rights seems to confirm rather than revise that judgment. That is why it is so important to investigate the origins of our Christian liberty and try to complete the often suppressed history of woman. This is being done with such matter-of-factness in the third world and with such self-confidence in the Anglo-Saxon world that we are challenged to take a critical look at our past so as not to leave our future to chance.

To deal with the question of women's rights is not a luxury of our time; it is a necessity in a changing society. That question also concerns the role of man, which has been made more one-sided, as well as the position of the child, who has become more insecure; it concerns economic problems and the shape of the church. To this extent, this volume also addresses men.

Each one of these topics needs a much more thorough treatment than any one person could give it in a short time. But if these essays provide not only stimulation and encouragement, but also impetus for further critical work, their goal will have been attained.

Woman in the New Testament

INTRODUCTION

The ancient world is known as a man's world, the world of patriarchy. Homer, Odysseus, Caesar, and Augustus made the history, filled the literature, and molded the shape of this world. Women in those days only attained fame if they acted out of character by committing some political, social, sexual, or other bit of extravagance. Few of their names are remembered, and their status as outsiders is typical.

Man played the dominant role in family, society, politics, and cult life. Reason, achievement, and strength were qualities that distinguished him from the allegedly more emotional, weaker, and therefore inferior woman. According to Aristotle, man is the most advanced form of human existence. Man, in accordance with nature, is, in relation to woman, like the better to the lesser good. And according to the Jewish philosopher Philo, "the position of man contains reason, but that of woman sensuality." Thus woman was altogether subordinated in society. On the farm she still enjoyed a certain independence through her work. But in the city, the development of the harem signified absolute slavery. Although this can be combined with chivalrous and verbal esteem, it does not alter the fact that in the sexual, social, and cultural realms woman was usually relegated to a restricted role.

The values and norms of society and culture in a patriarchal system are set by certain male attitudes. Since our world is also patriarchal to a great extent, it is difficult to envision norms outside the male norms. Nevertheless, recent research in cultural history has repeatedly drawn our attention to cultures stressing the rights of the mother (matriarchal) and their principles of liberty and equality, along with their feeling for nature, soil, and creaturely existence. We see cultures in which both woman and man mold behavior. Thus the distinguishing marks of patriarchal cultures are made even more obvious: having one's own way, dominance of the strong, competitiveness, achievement-oriented thinking, warlike aggressiveness, technical reasoning, one-sided predominance of reason over emotion, and will over impulse. The values commonly represented by woman, such as, for example, harmony, sense of community, tolerance, receptivity, spontaneity, creativity, emotion determining reason, occur only in the private realm or as compensation for the hardness of the male world.

Pure political matriarchies have probably never existed, but strong intrusions of new "feminine" elements and behavior patterns into mainly "male" cultures are known to have occurred now and then. They functioned as correctives or opened new cultural epochs. In our own history, the age of Romanticism was one of those times: feeling, Eros, and discourse created a new space and style for themselves and made the one-sided, rational age of Enlightenment more fruitful; they also prepared the way for a new social recognition of woman.

The time of Jesus and of the New Testament is another epoch when women—albeit only upper-class women—developed a new independence and culture, which was very important for the later history of the first Christian congregation.

Suppressed matriarchal desires and conceptions were again realized in the Hellenistic melting pot of many peoples, cultures, and religions. An emancipation of women was in progress which lasted until the second century after Christ. In the fourth century before Christ, Plato had already spoken of the fundamental ethical equality of woman, which should not, however, affect man's political dominance and the state's social structure. The philosophical schools of Stoicism and Neoplatonism had even demanded equality and monogamy. Thus, at the time of Christ, woman had, with the good will of the philosophers, achieved a position in society. She acquired an education, traveled alone, had the right to inherit property, and could attain recognition as, for example, the owner of a racing stable, a physician, or a business woman. In Rome, during the absence of their husbands, women celebrated a feast in honor of "the good goddess" from which men were excluded. The supremacy of man was put in doubt, even though there were violent arguments about it and public morality maintained the ideal of the assiduous and chaste housewife. Even the study of philosophy could be used to serve good housekeeping: "Only a woman well versed in philosophy can be a good housewife" (Musonius).

The social and cultural *structure* of society remained more or less untouched by the emancipation movement. There was a search for a "harmonious coexistence" and compatibility of interests, but a social revolution did not take place. And so, in practice, man remained the leading partner in marriage; spirit and body were not reconciled; and equality remained an abstract demand that collapsed when confronted with the social reality shaped by Roman law.

THE GOSPEL'S IRRUPTION INTO THE ANCIENT WORLD

Jesus

Jesus and his message must be seen against the background of the ancient world. Palestine, where Jesus made his appearance, was in no way the large world of progressive ideas, emancipated ladies, and sensible men who tolerated independent women. Palestine was a small conservative enclave in the progressive Roman empire of that time, where many cultures and religions mingled and where many different lifestyles were developed.

Jewish tradition and interpretations of the law still determined the people's consciousness and the customs of the country, despite some attempts at reform. The pious Jew still thanked God every morning that he was not an unbeliever, a slave, or a woman. Tradition said, "Woe unto him whose children are females." The world was divided into dominating male rationality and female emotion (Josephus). Women sat in the gallery of the synagogue and so never entered the inner sanctum of the house of God. The integrity of a worship service according to orthodox Jewish practice did not depend on whether or not women were present. Women were not permitted to say confession or thanksgiving prayers; only saying grace was allowed them. The Jewish patriarchy was severe, although some of its traits were favorable to woman. Naturally, there was no question of any emancipation of women.

This background makes Jesus' appearance and message even more impressive. Jesus broke his ties to his family even though, as the eldest of eight siblings, ?
he should have assumed the responsibility of caring

for the family after his father's death, according to
the tradition then in force. He encountered women as
well as men with complete naturalness and spontaneous matter-of-factness. He addressed both as
equals "in a partnership of objectivity," as though
differences and discrimination had never existed. It is
true that he never demanded emancipation, just as he
never called for a social revolution. But his speech
and his life contain a kind of dynamite which could
one day erase social barriers and the separation of the
sexes. Women are just as lonely and just as far from
God as men (Luke 7:36ff.); they are called to imitate
him and become his disciples just as much as men are
(Luke 8:2–3). How naturally Jesus entered their
homes (Luke 10:38–39), and how equally naturally
women violated tradition when they behaved like
disciples! For a woman even to serve at table was unthinkable to orthodox Jews. Occasionally a serving
woman did appear at the feet of the rabbi, but "a
female disciple, who only listens to the words of the
master, is unusual," according to the Jewish
philosopher Ben Chorin. A late Judaic saying was,
"May the words of the Torah be destroyed by fire
before they are delivered to the females!" Another
woman, roused to sudden ardor, demonstrated her
love for Jesus by pouring the most precious ointment
over his feet (Luke 7:36ff.).

According to recent historical research, Jesus

wandered through Palestine with men and at least six women. Conditioned by an almost two-thousand-year-old tradition, we are accustomed to picturing Jesus in the circle of twelve male disciples. The background is then composed of "serving women"—as our Bible translations so aptly phrase it—which we then quickly link to the institutional and congregational diaconate, thanks to our own ecclesiastical notions. The theologian and psychotherapist Hanna Wolff wrote, "We must thoroughly revise our notions regarding the group of disciples." She pointed out that the number twelve occurs frequently in the history of religions: twelve disciples of Buddha, for example. Moreover, this number was meant to represent symbolically the Old Testament tradition of the twelve tribes of Israel in the Christian tradition.

If one looks back beyond this Judeo-Christian revision and stylization, one meets a group of women who were just as significant as the male disciples to the life and death of Jesus and to the founding of the first Christian congregations. We know six names: *Joanna,* wife of one of King Herod's government officials; *Susannah,* a Jewess who was healed; *Mary,* wife of the disciple Cleopas; *Mary,* mother of James and Jesus; *Salome,* mother of the fishermen-disciples James and John; *Mary Magdalene,* who was healed and later played a leading role in the early church

(Mark 15:40; Luke 8:2ff.; 24:10; John 19:25). They
came from different social strata. On the whole, they
were wealthy, kept their wealth when they joined
Jesus' following, and then provided the group with a
certain amount of financial independence. A few of
them had been ill (probably mentally ill), and had remained among Jesus' followers after he healed them.
They can be distinguished from their male colleagues
by the fact that they were present at the execution of
Jesus and were not in the least afraid of being ar-
rested for complicity or membership in Jesus' group.
The "strong" men were still in hiding when the
women watched a wealthy city councilor bury Jesus.
And when the legal sabbath was over, they came with
ointments and balsam to do final honor to the dead
man. Not even the wife of the government official
hesitated to compromise herself for the dead traitor.
As for the married couple among the disciples, Mary
and Cleopas, we know that she stayed with the
women while he fled. Later, he was one of the Em-
maus disciples who encountered Jesus, and he was
well aware that the women had already seen Jesus.

It is the women who were the first to see the empty
tomb and to learn about the resurrection. Their
fearless and steadfast discipleship made them the
first "apostles," the first proclaimers of the Easter
message. This was never embodied in the ecclesiastical hierarchy, but, now and then, it has been

acknowledged as the first and true apostolate (by Bernard of Clairvaux, for example).

Jesus' Message

What made Jesus, his person and his message, so attractive to women in particular? (Americans today are asking, "Was Jesus a feminist?") Why did early Christendom already appear to be a "religion of slaves and women," as the pagan philosopher Celsus mockingly put it? Why is it that even today many more women than men fill the church pews?

Jesus calls the human being into a new being, free of anxiety and unconcerned about any personal or social pressures. This new human being lives solely by the sovereignty of grace, and is capable of giving this fearless existence space and form without compromise or concession. Oppressed and constricted people are, to begin with, more open to such a call than others who think they have more elbow room. Tax collectors, sick people, and women were the outsiders and victims of discrimination in society. But the call to freedom cannot be heard unless space for freedom has been created and the prison of discrimination has been opened. Jesus broke through the barriers, on behalf of Eastern women, by attacking the marriage laws then in force. He set the marriage that cannot be broken by adultery or divorce, and that is lived with one woman only, in place of Jewish

marriage practice in which polygamy and husband-
initiated divorce were possible. For him, even the in-
tention to commit adultery was already a sin before
God (Mark 10:10).

If we immediately tried to derive a law for our time
from this, we would misunderstand the new being into which Jesus intends to call us. These radical
demands are simultaneously radical promises made
to the person who lives in the carefree fellowship of
grace. "Sin no more" is the affirmation and promise
experienced by the acquitted adulteress.

Accordingly, both woman *and* man are responsible
for their marriage. To Jesus, however, marriage was
not a monopoly of Christian life, which is what many
Christians since the Lutheran Reformation have
made of it: the only lifestyle pleasing to God. To him
there are no marital relationships in heaven (Mark
12:25); he even had an almost hostile attitude toward
his own family, which tried to claim him for itself
(Mark 3:31ff.; Matt. 12:46ff.; Luke 8:19ff.; 14:26).
Blood ties are not decisive to the new, liberated existence; Jesus' relationship to his mother was up-
graded only in the course of tradition-history.

To the ancient world's understanding of tribe and
marriage—and perhaps to our own middle-class
sense of family as well—these are radical and
frightening expectations, unless we simultaneously
understand them as possibilities for a new style of

life. But Jesus' marriage reform—if one can call it that—remains a side product of his call to a life free of anxiety and aware of responsibility.

In order to grasp the significance of Jesus to the women of his time, we have to take one further step. Jesus called women to self-evident partnership with himself and others. He did not do so because he was a Humanist, feminist, or social reformer, but because he proclaimed a radically new experiencing of God—as Hanna Wolff has shown. He could make people new partners with each other because he let them experience God in a totally new and totally different way.

For the first time in the history of religions a God was proclaimed who does not measure according to religious achievement, property, or action, but rather is oriented toward the have-nothing, are-nothing, and can-do-nothing. To him the susceptible, the poor, the hungry, and the suffering are happy, saved, and blessed. Thus he turns all the values of this male-shaped world based on achievement, property, and action upside down. In their place he sets the receptive, tolerating, open methods of being most often embodied by women. "Jesus is the first man who broke through the androcentricity of the ancient world" (Hanna Wolff). In order to express what God does for humanity, he often used examples out of woman's life and behavior: the hen that protects her

chicks, the woman who searches for the lost coin.
Persistence, patience, perseverance in pursuing small
things, tirelessness, yes even unreasonableness—for
what could deserve such a commitment!—character-
ize the way God treats human beings. In the parables,
wherever God appears as a male figure, such as
father, banker, or employer, this role is never carried
through. The father, contrary to all normal patriarchal expectations, runs to the prodigal son; the
banker tears up the IOUs; the employer, contrary to
all contractual agreements, pays the person who did
practically no work. The parables of Jesus are full of
examples of how normal male behavior is violated by
unreasonable, unheard-of, unjust-seeming behavior.
Jesus' God-image is a challenge because of its em-
phasis on the female method of being and behavior.
Such methods of being and behavior are on the
fringes of the God-image in other religions, or else
they are rediscovered in special female Gods. But
these female and male behavior patterns are in-
tegrated in Jesus' God-image.

Time and again in the course of Christian history,
however, one-sided male God-images were moved into the center, arousing fear rather than effecting
liberation: God as judge, God as the one who
demands satisfaction; God who in Christ forgives
past sins but then simply places the human being at
point zero of a possible new moral start. Such a

calculating and frightening God often corresponded to a feminine, loving Jesus with whom the human being, rendered insecure, attempted to console himself. But this split God-image does not conform to the God Jesus proclaimed. His God forgives, not by calculating but by moving human beings into a new life. He does not desert human beings at point zero, but instead calls them into a new freedom. There is frequently a patriarchal misunderstanding when God is thought of in terms of finance and brokerage customs. Whenever God is understood as light, as life, as being, as the fullness of existence, one is a step closer to the truth of the freeing grace which makes us whole.

In an androcentric world, a world of achievement, legalism, action, and success, Jesus proclaimed a God who is not satisfied by achievement, negotiation, action, but rather liberates the senses and frees a new emotionality. He thereby opens a new space in which "reason and all the senses" come into their own and out of which responsible action results. He wants to penetrate and grasp the *whole* person, thus eliminating the split between reason and feeling, male and female behavior.

The Early Church

The new community was, therefore, a fellowship of women and men in which—in contrast to the

Jewish world around them—women were specifically given credit for decisive abilities. This soon led to their being entrusted with decisive functions. The first church, quickly spreading beyond the small conservative enclave of Palestine into the Hellenistic world, continued the new lifestyle as naturally as Jesus had done with it. The Hellenistic environment, favorable to emancipation, helped it to do so. Since women behaved in an independent manner, were well educated and professionally self-supporting, it was not surprising that women in the new Christian groups also behaved in a free and independent manner.

Women as individuals turned to the new faith (Acts 17:4); Paul preached to individual groups of women (for example, in Philippi, Acts 16:13); and women were particularly and repeatedly mentioned as listeners to his sermons. But women could also passionately oppose him (Acts 13:50), and were specifically mentioned as victims of Saul's persecution of Christians. If they had been persecuted solely as members of family groups, they would not have been named specifically. In Corinth they appeared self-confidently at worship services, in the new fashion of liberated women, with uncovered heads (1 Cor. 11). Of course this aroused debates as to how far such secular freedom should also be practiced in worship services. Many women stemmed from the upper classes and already enjoyed a certain amount of external and internal security; but many slave women were also repeatedly named as members of the inner circles of the church (Rom. 16:12; Acts 12:3).

Wherever there is so much independence, there is also the assumption of responsibility. We all know those women of the earliest church who were leaders of congregations meeting in homes. But we must not think of them as housewives in a modern family; instead we must see them as managers of average businesses. One of the most important functions of the earliest church—prophecy—cannot be conceived of without women. To Paul, this is the highest spiritual gift one can attain (1 Cor. 14). We must see this as the interpretive and proclaiming sermon within the church, in contrast to evangelization which was addressed to non-Christians. Philip's four daughters (Acts 21:9) and the women in Corinth represented such a relation of the gospel's reality to the life of the congregation. According to the prophecy of Joel (Joel 3:1), the Spirit is to be poured equally on men and women so that they can prophesy. Peter referred to this promise in his Pentecost sermon (Acts 2:17). Thus prophecy became a solid component of the early church and was appropriated by both women and men.

What has been said so far remains within the

framework of activities in the church, and can be understood on the basis of our own experience. But now new research has discovered that, in early Christianity, women worked at the apostles' side in an independent capacity in the mission field. This means that they worked in a risky and unusual field for the typical woman of that time. It can be demonstrated in certain passages that the "trouble" and "hard work" women like Tryphaena, Tryphosa, and Persis had (Rom. 16:6, 12) was in special mission work, in evangelization to the pagan environment.

Junias (Rom. 16:7)—in our Bible, a male companion of Paul's, an earlier apostle than Paul, and a fellow prisoner—must have been the famous female apostle named "Junia." Later, one believed no woman capable of being a prisoner, an early apostle, or a friend of Paul's, and so one made her a man or the wife of the Andronicus named in the same passage. Since the Enlightenment, she has definitely been known as the man named "Junias."

Paul certified that Euodia and Syntyche engaged in missionary "battle" (Phil. 4:2-3), a strong word that can in no way be linked to housekeeping or charity contributions in the mission field. Priscilla, in addition to her husband Aquila, Paul, Barnabas, and Apollo, was a leading figure in mission to the Gentiles and Apollo's teacher (Acts 18:26, according to Chrysostom). Out of the six times she is mentioned, she is named before her husband four times. She was a business woman, a tent manufacturer; and she traveled widely on business affairs. The famous theologian Harnack considered her and her husband to be the authors of the Epistle to the Hebrews.

Another traveling business woman was the well-known Phoebe (Rom. 16:1), often considered to be the first deaconess. Theodor Fliedner believed that the office of deaconess derived from her, and she is to this day falsely understood as "Mother of the Congregation" and as "parish aide." But one should really think of her as a traveler on an international European train rather than as a wearer of the deaconness cap in Kaiserswerth. Her titles of "deacon" and "superintendent" point to a responsible position of bishop, elder, or deacon, which she occupied in the Corinthian port city of Cenchreae. The letter of recommendation she received legitimized her as a coworker in mission work. She thus seems to have exercised all the functions of a top official in the Christian community.

The above-mentioned Mary Magdalene, or Mary of Magdala, must have been a leading figure of authority in the first Palestinian congregation. Later sources report disputes over authority between her and the disciples—especially Peter—which already point to the later patriarchal regression from this first springtime.

The fascinating and novel aspect of these women is not only that they held their own in a Hellenistic environment favorable to women, but also that they could freely develop their talents in the company of men in a religious group. That women and men could live and work side by side for about fifty years in the first community cannot be explained solely sociologically on the basis of the environment favorable to emancipation; rather, one must above all explain it on the basis of Jesus' saving message about the wholeness of a human being. Of course the feminism of the time was a help and offered the possibility of starting the experiment of a fellowship of women and men.

THE NEW TESTAMENT
Paul

Why was it the silent female and not the female bishop who made history? Why doesn't the women's movement come through as clearly in the Bible as I have just portrayed it?

The feminist tradition of the early churches only protrudes into the Bible "like the tip of an iceberg" (Elisabeth Schussler). Again and again attempts have been made to plumb the size of this iceberg. Large contributions toward this end were made by German neo-Protestantism at the turn of this century and by the American feminist movement of today. Sociology, psychology, and American feminist literary criticism have advanced us a decisive step. For in the Bible as we know it, the feminine tradition can only be seen filtered through a patriarchal revision. Yet the Bible has still been able, in spite of it all, to operate as a revolutionary potential.

Paul, who had such impressive female coworkers, and whose work would probably not have been possible without them, is an example of how difficult it is to forget an education shaped by men. He was absolutely convinced that in Christ there is no difference between man and woman. Galatians 3:28 is the decisive passage in which he made clear that the old Jewish separation between peoples, social groups, and men and women no longer existed in the new community. This was also a central point of the gospel for the learned rabbi. But when it came to questions of style and behavior, elements of patriarchal thought patterns on order kept oozing out of him—elements which had not yet been assimilated by his new insight. Thus, in conformity with the custom of the earliest church, he conceded prophecy to the Corinthian ladies; but at the same time he stumbled over the new-fashioned custom of doing so without a head covering. He argued this custom in terms of the God-Christ-man-woman order, with one being the head of the other and woman being the last and weakest limb (also in Eph. 5:22ff.; Col. 3:18ff.; 1

Pet. 3:1ff.; Tit. 2:5ff.), but immediately relativized this with the idea that in Christ man and woman are one, after all. He, as well as many Christians to this day, found it difficult to draw social consequences from spiritual insight. He found his female co-workers already there, and so accepted them. But he was frightened of the feminist customs in the congregations, reacted defensively, and retreated to custom, law, and order. Today, there is general doubt that he originated the fateful sentence that a female should keep silent in the congregation; nor does this sentence accord with the congregational practice of his time or with his basic conviction. But it cannot be assumed either that he particularly promoted women; in any case, he addressed the *brothers* in his letters. Sisters, who constituted a third of his coworkers, were named only in individual cases. The fellowship of women and men had already turned into the church of brothers as it exists to this day.

A momentous development on still one other point can be traced back to Paul. Marriage was, to Paul, a necessary evil: to marry is good, but not to marry is better. He himself, unmarried out of principle because of his apostolate and his anticipation of the imminent irruption of God's kingdom, drew a "dark picture of marriage" (Cancik), in sharp contrast to his pagan environment with its pleasure in sensuality and eroticism. To Paul, marriage is only the realm where sexual appetites are satisfied. "All the cheerful half-notes that define what is human are so painfully missing: tenderness, beauty, naturalness, high-mindedness, nobility, gaiety . . . " (Cancik).

Whereas no ascetic tendencies can be demonstrated in Jesus, the first contrasts between "spiritual" and "sexual" show up in Paul. Flesh, sin, and lust are often lumped together, and thus the beginning is made for a momentous development in the church: the contempt for, and satanization of, sexuality.

Even the Reformers still combined sexual drives and sin. Luther married "to outwit the devil." He considered marriage a "hospital to treat the plagues of sexual urges." Calvin married "for the sake of weak flesh." Only today does one begin to understand body, desires, and sexuality as essential components of the wholeness of a person. But the old hostility to sex and body still exists subconsciously in Christian thinking.

Synoptic Gospels

The Gospels were written about twenty years later. They mirror how, on Palestinian soil, woman had been freed from the traditional patriarchal bonds and had become a full-fledged member of the early church. If, in the Old Testament, God's patriarchal covenant-relationship with male heirs had favored man, if marriage had acquired its meaning through male heirs, and marital practices (marriage with the maid) were adjusted accordingly, and if Abraham's *sons* were known as the bearers of the promise, then now Abraham's *daughters* were also inserted into the succession of salvation (Luke 13:16). Later, a revolutionary thesis was rumored about Jesus: that he had also instituted daughters as heirs! Such a violation of tradition could already be found occasionally in reformatory Jewish circles, but the break with the tradition of the fathers—the old covenant—in favor of a completely new fellowship of all the disinherited only became visible in the Palestinian Christian churches.

To Mark and Matthew, women were *one* fringe group like other fringe groups—heathens, criminals, tax collectors, and the poor—who constituted the church.

To the physician Luke, who had a special interest in the social integration of the poor, in society's recognition of the church, and in Hellenistic emancipation, women were an extremely important group whose needs had heretofore been mostly overlooked. He therefore composed his gospel in a cleverly pedagogical way and set up a frequent man-woman balance: he set the prophetess Hannah next to the prophet Simeon (Luke 2); the story of the widow of Nain follows the story of the captain of Capernaum; the good Samaritan is followed by the story about Mary and Martha. The crippled woman is healed because she is Abraham's daughter, and the tax collector Zacchaeus experiences salvation because even a transgressor of the law is a descendant of Abraham (Luke 13:16; 19:9). If Mark and Matthew already had a few parallel stories addressed to man and woman in their different spheres of life—for example, the man sows the mustard seed and the woman bakes bread (Matt. 13:31–33)—then Luke added new examples that fascinated his female audiences: if God's way of searching for human beings is made clear to man, in the first two Gospels, through the example of the lost sheep, then the same thing is now demonstrated to woman with the example of the lost coin (Luke 15). He combined the pleading widow with the praying tax collector (Luke 18). Unfortunately, Paul's militant and athletic images of the runner and the fighter have found more adherents in Christian proclamation than the gospel writers', especially Luke's, domestic images.

The disciples' anger over Jesus' unconventional behavior with women was also captured in the Gospels: the irritated disciples tried to guard their master against women's spontaneous importunities; they found it irksome that children who, due to nature's necessity, do after all belong to women, must now be dragged along; female extravagance was criticized, the Easter experience was laughed at as imaginative female fabrication and was not believed.

To be sure, the decisive factor for later tradition-history is that cuts were made in the earliest Christian feminist tradition. A tendency to play down the role of women as witnesses and proclaimers of the Easter kerygma became visible in all the gospel accounts of the disciples' reaction to the women's Easter experience. According to Mark, the women kept silent "out of fear"; according to Luke, the disciples thought it was "chatter." And then came the more creditable male substitute story of Jesus' appearance to Peter (Luke 24:34). In many regions, this Peter tradition seems to have displaced the feminist tradition quite early. For instance, Paul does not seem to have known any other (1 Cor. 15:4–5). In John, Peter and John are correspondingly played off against the Mary Magdalene tradition.

In spite of the prominent position occupied by woman in the first three Gospels, patriarchal revision can be recognized which acknowledged the twelve male disciples—but not, in the same way, the female disciples—as bearers of tradition and as congregational leaders. In the fellowship of women and men, men have already occupied the leading positions and the original tradition has clearly been corrected. In the churches themselves, in their composition and style, the revolutionary potential was still alive.

The Gospel of John

The Gospel of John, written very late (A.D. 90–100), presents an exception. According to the latest research done by an American Jesuit, it is a heretofore almost totally ignored source for a very independent feminist tradition in the Johannine churches of Asia Minor. Paul's vision of "no Jew, no Greek, neither slave nor free, neither man nor woman" did not remain a dream here, but was realized to a much greater extent than in the Pauline congregations. A subordinated woman would have been unthinkable here. Even the foot-washing that Jesus performed for his disciples—actually a wife's intimate service for her husband, recounted only by John—seems to be an action symbolizing the new order: the master takes over woman's servant role.

Right at the beginning of Jesus' activity, the Samaritan woman (John 4) received a commission to do mission which is once more reminiscent of the participation of women in the founding of these churches. The tradition of the twelve male disciples, which was already dominant in the gospel too, was repeatedly softened by other people seemingly more important to the church: the disciple "beloved by Jesus" who clearly competed with Peter; and the two women, Mary and Martha, who were also "beloved" by Jesus and treated with special distinction (John 11:5).

The confession of Christ, spoken by Peter in the Synoptic Gospels, is here attributed to Martha (Matt. 16:16; John 11:27). It is emphasized that Mary Magdalene was a witness to the resurrection *before*

Peter was. Thus the probably prevalent tradition, known also to Paul (1 Cor. 15:5), that Peter was the first to see the Lord, is revised. Peter did come to the tomb, but it was Mary Magdalene who experienced the first revelation of the resurrection. Jesus called her by name and thus called her into discipleship, into "his own." Her pronouncement, "I have seen the Lord" (John 20:18), was the expression of the legitimization of the apostolate in the Pauline congregations too. Thus, in the face of growing clericalization in the church, a very independent and vital feminist tradition was able to survive much longer in these churches of Asia Minor than in other regions.

Pastoral Epistles

The Jesus-tradition became more and more diluted, and the false patriarchal understanding of Jesus grew larger and larger in the Pastoral Epistles (Timothy, Titus, Peter). Was the dynamite of equality still present, and would it become explosive?

The first, earliest Christian burning anticipation of the imminent end had been extinguished by this time. The kingdom of God had not broken in, and the charismatic male and female leaders of the congregations had been replaced by officials. External dangers threatened: persecution of young Christianity; Gnosis, a dangerous worldview which denied the value of all physical and earthly existence; and groups of enthusiasts who created schisms.

The early church at this time followed the never-quite-replaced ancient conservative ideas of order, and developed a juridical-political concept of office and authority. In order to survive, it adapted itself as much as possible to its environment and adopted its social forms. The most important factor in a patriarchal environment is the search for one's own patriarch. So the office of bishop was arrived at, and this office was from now on reserved exclusively to men. Gone were the days of female apostles, prophetesses, and deaconnesses who led congregations. The bishop had to have the identity of a married man, a good husband and a good father. Celibacy was no longer taken into account either. And so the bishop represented ecclesiastical and domestic patriarchy. The days of the earliest Christian fellowship of women and men were gone.

A female position of leadership had no place in patriarchal forms like these, so woman was pushed back into the home. But a remnant of the early charismatic beginnings remained: an *office of widow* was developed out of the leadership position held by women; this office of widow assigned deaconly duties to the widow who was left uncared-for and without family, was sixty years old, and enjoyed a spotless reputation. In those days, when widows lacked any rights or duties and were regarded as belonging to the lower class, this was an important social contribution—a sign that Jesus' dynamite could still be effective. At the same time, it guaranteed better care for the women in the congregations. But the leadership position of women was now confined to praying (1 Tim. 5:5) and teaching other women, and was thus reduced to an office of women for women.

The newly created female functions in the churches of the twentieth century—women's aide, parish worker, women's world day of prayer—mirror the already patriarchal phase of the early church, not its charismatic beginnings. The new office created at that time—as important as it was—lost its totality of reference, separated the sexes, and brought heretofore unknown ascetic tendencies to the leadership position of women. It was explicitly stressed that the widow is an older woman, beyond the age of sexual needs (1 Tim. 5:11). It was argued that young widows could follow their sexual desires rather than Jesus. Nor was the married woman, as Priscilla had been in the earliest church, any longer qualified for office. Spiritual office and feminine sexuality became opposites.

If early signs of ascetic tendencies showed up in the person of the apostle Paul, now female leadership position and female sexuality had become irreconcilable. Flesh, desire, drives, and passion were realms delivered up to Satan or the Evil One because they are uncontrollable. The alternatives to the leadership position of women were now either Christ or sex.

Only marriage could create "peace, discipline, and order"; outside of marriage, the Christian existence of young women was constantly threatened. At this point, the Jewish idea—which had been overcome in the early Christian tradition—resurfaced: Eve was the first to sin and that is why she is inferior to man (1 Tim. 2:13ff.; see also Ecclus. 25:24; Eccles. 7:27). By way of the church fathers and St. Augustine, this idea has determined Christian tradition for centuries and still exists subconsciously in Protestantism. In this way, male sexual difficulties, feelings of inferiority and guilt were projected onto woman. Only the human being determined by will and consciousness at the very core of his/her person could be considered healthy in the ancient world. Not until today has it become clear to us that only the total human being—a being with drives and will—is a whole, true human being; and that just so, with his/her conscious and his/her subconscious, does a human being know him/herself accepted by God.

An interesting aspect of this development is what Christian tradition did to the first female apostle, Mary of Magdala. The story that her mental illness was cured by Jesus (Luke 8) was linked to the story of the great sinner (Luke 7). Sin and mental illness were blended and projected as sexual guilt onto one female person, and out came the portrait of the great penitent Mary Magdalene which entered art, literature, and Roman Catholic liturgy. Thus was created a necessary corrective image to the perfection of Mary, the other woman-image. But no trace was left of Mary of Magdala, the first female apostle.

The subordination of woman was now derived from an order of being that classified woman as fundamentally inferior. In Paul, in his Epistles to the Ephesians and Colossians, the subordination could still be understood as a dynamic one, deriving from an order of Christ in which *each* person is subordinated to the other (for example, Eph. 5:21). But the typical Christian woman was now the good housewife dependent on her husband, occupied with bearing and raising children, unobtrusive, without much jewelry but well dressed, and never smarter than her husband. She no longer contributed anything to the congregation except her silent presence and, in old age, her social and charitable services to other women. It is true that there always had been housewives limited to a small circle even in the earliest congregations, but now this type of woman had become the Christian norm which has shaped our church structures for almost two thousand years. This does not accord with Jesus' attitude toward women; nor does it accord with what was still possible with Paul and in the Johannine congregations. The house rules now matched, almost word for word, the similar tracts for housewives in the Hellenistic environment, insofar as these were not affected by the emancipation wave of the upper class.

Christendom adapted itself to lower middle-class conditions. The dynamite was defused.

A fraction of explosive material was nevertheless preserved. If one compares the contemporary Hellenistic tracts for housewives with those for Christians, it becomes apparent that the Hellenistic ones recommended the husband to treat his wife well for economic, natural law, or common sense reasons. The Christian husband, on the other hand, was exhorted to honor his wife because she too was "joint heiress to the life of grace" (1 Pet. 3:7).

The idea of love and religious equality softened the patriarchal system. This idea no longer had any social and ecclesiastical consequences, as it had had with Jesus, Paul, and John, but perhaps it made the daily routine of marriage a little friendlier and helped woman achieve inner sovereignty.

Traces of the impressive social standing of women, derived from religious equality in the early church, are still visible in the New Testament. A retreat to lower-middle-class ideas of order, conditioned by the environment, is obvious in the later writings. But the dynamite—the message about the same grace for woman and man—was preserved to become explosive time and again in the course of history.

Four Stations on the Road to Woman's Coming of Age

I. INTELLECTUAL-POLITICAL COMING OF AGE

The question of human emancipation and coming of age arose with the Enlightenment. At that time, it was recognized that a human being could be characterized by reason and will. In addition came the discovery of things that had kept human beings immature: the state, society, and above all the church and religion, which had demanded adaptation, subordination, and obedience. To reason, to use one's mind, had been forbidden. Obedience was the structure of life. In his famous essay "What Is Enlightenment?" the German philosopher Kant explained, "Enlightenment is the human being's way out of self-imposed immaturity. . . . Immaturity is the inability to use one's mind without someone else's guidance. . . . Have the courage to make use of your own intellect!"

Freedom of intellect, which had perhaps existed in-
dividually and in private, was now to be exercised
publicly. This concerned the officer who had
heretofore said, "Don't use your brains, drill!"; the
economic adviser who declared, "Don't use your intellect, pay!"; the pastor, who usually said, "Don't
use your reason, believe!" The use of intellect in
public opened up a new order of society: a society of
the critically free and equal.

But the right to come of age was demanded above
all by people of the ruling class, and at that time this
meant men. It is true that, in theory, Kant encouraged all human beings to come out of their self-imposed immaturity. But then he sneered that "the pre-
ponderance of humanity (including the whole gentle
sex)" found it very comfortable to be immature,
because the book thinks for me, the pastor is my conscience, and the doctor prescribes my diet. Church
and tradition had first made people "as stupid as
domestic animals" to keep them nice and quiet, and
had then painted a picture for them of how dangerous it was "to take free steps away from the
walker."

Thus Kant's mockery of the immaturity of his con-
temporaries applied partly to men, but generally to
women. Today, it is thought that although he knew
everything that occurred between the starry heavens
above us and the moral law within us, he nevertheless

spoke about women "like a vulgar propagandist for antifeminism" (Hanna Wolff). His opponent, the philosopher Hamman, countered in his day that "he looks askance at self-imposed immaturity in just the same way as he looks askance at the whole gentle sex, and my three daughters won't sit still for it." Kant did not think much of women: "When I was young and could have used a woman, I could not feed her. When I was old and could have fed one, I had no use for her." To him, marriage was an institution wherein woman attains her freedom and man loses his.

A similar discrepancy between theoretical insight and practical application can be found in Rousseau. He did indeed write that the human being is born free, but it became quite clear in most of his writings and in his treatment of his wife that this did not apply to women.

Thus man had the chief opportunities to come of age, specifically ruling-class man, insofar as he had the "courage" to flout convention. There is some thing elitist about "coming of age." Intellect, logic, persistence, the loneliness of courage and isolation from others are demanded. We would today designate them as so-called typical male attitudes, which contrast with the so-called female attitudes like adaptability, coordination, tolerance, sense of community, and spontaneity. Kant's hostility to women is not just a personal oddity, it also seems to have taken its bearings from the patriarchal standards of his time.

But there soon appeared Enlightenment poets and philosophers like Gellert, Lessing, and Wolff who were favorable to women and who demanded equal status and equal education for girls. The next generation consciously began to integrate women into the newly opened world of reason and will. The theologian Schleiermacher—influenced by the Zinzendorf brand of Pietism, which credited the "sister," too, with intellectual talent—led the way and composed a *Catechism of Reason for Noble Women*. The second article of the creed reads, "I believe in the power of the will and of education to bring me closer to the Infinite again, to free me from the bonds of false education, and to make me independent of the barriers to my sex." The first schools for girls were founded, at first for upper-class girls who were intended to become equal intellectual conversation-partners for enlightened men, then later for girls of the middle class. At first maturity was practiced in upper-class salons, and then one began to demand suffrage for all female citizens. The process of Enlightenment proceeded from the top downward: it began with ruling-class men, grasped their wives, and then all levels of the middle class. The presupposition was a certain financial security, a class of society that permitted education, and an atmosphere that favored the training of the will.

In the course of time, many educational possibilities and many careers were opened up to the new woman. She was permitted to bring forth the highest scientific achievements, which would even be acknowledged as hers. She could, as in past generations, engage in practical and charitable activities, but now she was more independent and possessed well-founded expertise. She had become independent of her family and its economic status. She was allowed to make judgments and to participate in politics. She fulfilled what the Enlightenment had demanded: liberation from immaturity. But was this new freedom, in which our unmarried aunts and great-aunts reveled, freedom for all? Weren't our married mothers and grandmothers, for example, as well as all lower-class women, excluded? Maturity was intended for all women of all classes and ties, but, in practice, only single women of the middle class profited from it because a new society and a new professional world opened itself only to them.

The case of Helen Lange—her personality and life—discloses the way intellectual-political coming of age still fell short of many wishes and dreams for a wholistic existence. Helen Lange was a late child of the Enlightenment. She heard about Kant and his *Critique of Pure Reason* when she was eighteen years old. She wanted to buy the book in her home town of Oldenburg, but the book was unknown there and had to be ordered, which caused a sensation and started gossip about her. Her dream was to obtain the same intellectual enlightenment as men. The way she achieved this was through a girl's high school, a high school certificate—she attained it after a tenacious struggle—and finally admission to the university and political suffrage. Her demands on herself and others to free themselves from "self-imposed immaturity" were high, which led to an overemphasis on clear objectivity and which left the impression of a lack of warm personal engagement. Julie Vogelstein remembered, "She let no one forget she had studied Greek." Unapproachable in bearing and dress, cool blue eyes, a tall figure—everything personal, intimate, or passionate was suppressed in her. Her autobiography starts with a lively description of her youth in Oldenburg, then the personal element is suddenly dropped, and the rest of the book is a biography of the feminist movement. Where were her sufferings and passions, her male and female friends, her conflicts and outbursts, her family life?

For a long time, the early feminist movement cultivated a somewhat arrogant academic flair alien to the imprint suffering made on other women in other situations. The exertions necessary to include woman's intellectual coming of age into a male intellectual world impoverished, constricted, and demanded sacrifices. Was there perhaps something more than the mind's coming of age after all? The "sexually neuter type woman" (Else Hoppe), undisturbed by husband, children, drives, passions, and financial difficulties, had begun to lead woman out of her "self-imposed immaturity."

II. ECONOMIC COMING OF AGE

The ideals of enlightened middle-class liberal emancipation had become suspect to many people at the time of a growing industrialization and an increasing number of workers dependent on wages. Weren't freedom, education, and maturity, in the final analysis, only the freedom of a few privileged people? Absolute rulers, who muzzled intellectual freedom, had been joined by industrial corporations which brought the masses into totally different dependencies.

The struggle against this new immaturity began with Karl Marx. In 1844, he stated that now the owners of the means of production were the "guardians" once named by Kant; they and their capital kept workers dependent. Expanding the Kantian ideas, he demanded "a categorical imperative to overthrow all conditions keeping a human being a degraded, enslaved, rejected, and contemptible creature." The fact that in these economic conditions women were particularly degraded and despised creatures did not yet pose a problem to him. His life was a typical late-middle-class mixture of an upright married life with a rich noblewoman and sexual affairs wherein the affected, degraded women and children seemingly caused him no suffering.

But Frederick Engles and, above all, August Bebel saw clearly that lower-class woman, especially the working woman, belonged in a double sense to these degraded and despised creatures. Therefore, for them the battle against economic guardianship was also a battle for woman's coming of age. As laborers, women at the time worked eleven-hour days. After deduction for rent, their daily wage was fifty to sixty pennies. Maids were required to work up to sixteen hours a day; domestic practice permitted the caning of maids. Literature contains repeated descriptions of the wretchedness of female servants. To woman's subordination to man, appropriate to the time, was added her economic exploitation by industry, thus creating a double load for her to bear.

Socialists had pointed out a new dimension of maturity: the coming of age that rests upon economic independence. A human being should not be liberated from work but from exploitation. Man's work in production and the economic independence thus gained should also shape woman's life. Only in this way could she actively participate in political and social life. The problems of frustrated Nora in *A Doll's House* (Ibsen) were characteristic of a middle-class existence; the mass of women did not encounter these problems in their own life struggles. For the middle-class feminist movement, a career was a matter for single women. Now, it seemed that all women involved in the process of production had a right to the true economic and political coming of age.

The "question of ladies' rights" replaced the "question of women's rights." Economic emancipation intended to liberate more completely. Marx had declared, "The dissolution of private property is the emancipation of all the senses and of all abilities." And Bebel described the new woman:

> The woman of the new society is totally independent socially and economically; she is no longer subject to even a trace of exploitation or mastery; she confronts man as a full and free equal; she is the mistress of her fate. Her education is the same as man's, with the exception of those deviations conditioned by the differences of sex and sexual function. Living a life conformable to nature, she can develop and use her physical and intellectual abilities as she wills. . . . Just now a factory worker, she is at another time of day educator, teacher, nurse; at a third time she may work at some kind of art or pursue a science, and at a fourth time she may be functioning as an administrator.[1]

In the German feminist movement at the end of the last century, a new, multifaceted, "sexually

1. August Bebel, *Die Frau und der Socialismus* (Berlin, 1964).

liberated" type of woman had appeared beside the
unmarried, intellectual teacher type.

Lily Braun, for example—daughter of a Berlin
general, at one time the emperor's playmate, much
admired by society, and heretofore passionately
engaged in the middle-class feminist movement—
switched at this time to the Socialist Women's movement. At the last common congress, she bitterly ac-
cused her middle-class sisters:

> The middle-class feminist movement's understanding
> for the question of women workers' rights can be
> most plainly demonstrated by the fact that, for my
> lecture about these workers—who encompass the
> great majority of the female sex, and who are the most
> disenfranchised and the most unhappy—I was alloted
> the same fifteen minutes as was alloted to the question
> of ladies' rights in girls' high schools. But perhaps it
> will dawn on you that there is a greater and more grip-
> ping wretchedness than that of the jobless and
> dissatisfied daughters of your class; that, outside your
> circles, a battle is being fought that is more serious
> and more sacred than the battle over a doctor's
> degree; and that the vitality of enthusiasm and the
> heroic courage of sacrifice can only be found where
> men and women use their combined strength to
> achieve the one great goal: everyone's liberation from
> economic and moral slavery.[2]

She herself united her active work in the Socialist

2. Lily Braun, *Memoiren einer Sozialisten* (Berlin, undated).

party with a passionate Dionysian existence. As with Clara Zetkin—the leader of the Socialist Women's movement, whose second husband was the painter Frederick Zundel—art and science, motherhood and profession were combined in Lily Braun's life.

Both women were passionate mothers. For the sake of her two sons, Clara Zetkin remained in provincial Stuttgart, even though she was the leader of the Socialist Women's movement as well as a leader in the Social-Democrat party, with headquarters in Berlin. Lily Braun's son, Otto, was one of those world-famous child prodigies who cannot be conceived of without a large measure of parental devotion. He was killed in battle in 1918, and influenced a whole generation with the posthumous publication of his *Writings of an Early Bloomer*. Because of her personal experiences, her efforts on behalf of women were total and encompassed an education which not only was academic but also covered the arts, business, and family. Both women were aware of the new problems of sexual needs and freedom of the body that were affecting the economically liberated woman, but they could not yet offer solutions to these problems. The Socialist type of woman seemed to be searching more comprehensively and more totally for her coming of age.

Only one thing did not fit into these calculations: equality of man and woman was illusion, not reality. The removal of the barriers making one human being dependent upon another, which Bebel had called for, had not been accomplished in any way, even by the leading comrades. Anyone who witnessed the social life of the Social-Democrat leaders could see that a Socialist party at the Bebel home, for instance, was in no way distinguishable from middle-class festivities: giggling women interested in recipes and the price of meat but not in party work or strikes. After dinner, men and women separated, and the respectable middle-class conversation was, "What do you think of Ibsen?" "Obey and darn socks" was the usual word both at home and in party work, and Bebel relegated child-rearing to the female sex, just as middle-class society did. The conflict of roles and its social consequences were not reflected upon. The optimistic hope was that, in the new Socialist society, the "nature" of man and woman could unfold fully. A lifestyle conformable to nature and the satisfaction of needs seemed guaranteed in a society of the no-longer-exploited. Bebel did not yet see the psychological factors of the old sex differentiations in their social consequences, and Lenin swept all these problems completely under the rug, since he found "the rooting about in sexual things" deeply offensive. He considered the Freudian theory, which understood false attitudes about sex to be the cause of neuroses, "a foolish fad" that "grew luxuriantly on the manure piles of middle-class society."

Liberated from economic guardians, the human

being nevertheless remained a creature molded only by will and reason, shaped by the Enlightenment. The economic liberation of the whole being, and therefore the liberation of its senses and corporal existence, was expected to be the automatic result of the economic alteration of society. No one was interested in the fact that the body has its own laws and its own needs, which, if suppressed, have emotional consequences and prevent the total liberation of a human being. The sexual revolution did not take place; wherever it was tolerated, as in the USSR at the beginning, it soon stumbled over outmoded models and economic difficulties, and it was soon banned by the government.

The family unit, still patriarchally shaped, had outlasted all social revolutions. The comrades proved to be pashas in state and family. The patriarchal state either prohibited or permitted abortions, depending on the economic situation; no particular value was put on woman's personality, corporal existence, or sexuality; woman's coming of age was dealt with on the basis of economics. The authority of the state and the outmoded patriarchal forms of society left woman no space of her own in the hierarchy. Only the right to work, the right to an education, and the respect society pays to the working woman were left, after the start of a new whole person and the dream of the "naturalization of the human being and the humanization of nature" (Marx).

III. SOCIAL COMING OF AGE

The course of Socialism, the experiment that was
to produce the woman come-of-age, was unsatisfac-
tory. Women in Socialist countries were more acknowledged, more respected, and more self-con-
fident than women in other countries of the Western
world, but they were more tired, "even more tired
than those in the Western world" (Beauvoir). A new
Soviet sociological analysis confessed that
"Socialism could not remove all the elements of fac-
tual inequality between man and woman." In the
West, one also accepted the "dual role of woman":
work and family. But the double load women had to
bear remained the same both in the East and West.
And the complaint of a Cologne feminist group,
"We are minors in both work and family," made obvious that a new phase in the struggle to achieve
maturity had begun in the sixties. It was a battle for
maturity that has parallels in the liberation struggles
of non-whites and other minority groups: woman
wanted to determine her own life, to realize herself,
to develop herself, and not to be man's appendage,
part-time help in the labor field or mediator in the
family any longer. Of what use is education if she
needed it only to help the children with homework?
Of what use is vocational training if she could not
have a career? Of what use is financial independence
if she no longer knew the limitations of her body and

became ill from the double load she bore? On the heels of intellectual-political and economic coming of age, the social coming of age was now the focal point of the discussion: full integration as an individual into society.

The guardians of the social bondage of women were harder to discover. They stick deep in society's traditions and in psychological prejudice regarding woman's nature and role, and regarding the division of powers according to which the world has been ruled for thousands of years. According to this division of powers, it is man who governs, rules, and shapes. Woman conceives, bears, and is responsible for home and children. Her "nature" urges this role on her, and this "conception of nature" holds woman in invisible bonds even in highly developed industrial nations.

How could woman be freed from such biological chains? How could it be made clear that this nature of woman, which had become tradition, reenslaved her despite all the seeming maturity? This was the theme which has worried the theoreticians of the feminist movement to this very day, and which is the theme of the Western world. It began with Simone de Beauvoir's famous book *The Second Sex* (1949), continued with Betty Friedan's *The Feminine Mystique* (1963), and was temporarily concluded with Kate Millet's standard work *Sexual Politics* (1970). This last book has been compared to Karl Marx's *Capital* and placed in the ranks of the great enlightening works about the guardians of our society.

Sigmund Freud had said that anatomy is fate, and so once again nailed down woman's old biological role for the otherwise enlightened middle class, despite all the movements for emancipation. Thus once again, unintentionally, the social division of labor was confirmed, and the phenomenon "woman" was explained with the psychic attitudes of passivity, masochism, and narcissism. The theory of female penis envy completed the impression of a female being who is formless nature, takes its bearings from man and his "possession," and is not an independent bearer of culture.

Simone de Beauvoir countered the often quoted lapidary sentence "Anatomy is fate" with the equally lapidary sentence "One is not born a women, one becomes a woman." If the early feminist movement had outwitted the problem of nature by setting woman's intellectual sovereignty above all physical-psychical aspects, if Socialist woman had crowded out the problem, then now Simone de Beauvoir stepped forward to fight decisively against all "friends of nature," all worshipers of motherhood, and all apostles of the eternal role distinction of the sexes. She was well armed: since the twenties, the American anthropologist Margaret Mead had been making research trips to unknown South Sea islanders, and had brought back the revolutionary findings that what in our culture we call "woman" and designate as "female" characteristics and activities are, in several cultures, characteristics of man. For example, among the Arapesh people the father takes over the nurturing role in a child's infancy.

"Nature," especially after Margaret Mead's research, had turned out to be something neutral, very easily influenced and very dependent. Accordingly, woman "is not a creation of nature, but a product of civilization." Every woman lives at a specific historical time and in a specific culture, and is dependent on them. But she must, according to Simone de Beauvoir, seize the freedom "to choose transcendence," to adjust to the values which man has created for such a long time in her society. Theoretically, she still has the possibility of choosing "alienation"—that is, to remain tied to her body like an animal. But the true definition of a human being is "freedom of action." Man has opened this future to which woman can now also rise. The new way demands courage and decisiveness, for it is easier to remain in the old passive family role. However, there are difficulties along this new road: education, which attempts to keep girls "feminine"; society, which conserves laws and prejudices to keep women dependent and subordinate; and finally man himself, who desires to remain "autonomous subject."

Simone de Beauvoir, whose story is already nearly

a legend, is today the grand old lady of the feminist
movement. She always *did* the unconventional, inap-
propriate thing: she was enthusiastic about the USSR
even in Stalin's day; she supported Existentialism
when it contradicted her Socialism; as a middle-class
lady, she marched arm in arm with students during
the Paris student riots of the sixties; unmarried, she
has been living for years with the philosopher Sartre,
even in the days when everyone was married. And she
always did these things with upper-middle-class bearing, her hair pinned up, and wearing conventional
dress, just as she had been trained to do as a child.
Bubbling nature contradicted the style. She subdued
nature, for, to her, nature, corporeality, is passive,
controlled by hormones, and always an obstacle to
freedom. To her, there are no positive possibilities in
being "body," and thus artificial insemination
seemed to her to be, in the distant future, the solution
to the problem of womanhood and motherhood. At
the moment, she considers children woman's "most
horrible enslavement." Her courage to demand
maturity from nature exacted its price.

The tenacity with which the theory of "woman's
nature" and her "natural duties" has lasted and even
prevailed, in spite of all the waves of emancipation,
was demonstrated fourteen years after de Beauvoir's
Second Sex in Betty Friedan's book *The Feminine
Mystique.* Women had long ago attained equal
rights, recognition, and admission to all professional

positions in the United States, when a new feminine
mystique overthrew all of women's intellectual and
political independence. Freud's saying about
anatomy as fate and his description of the female
psyche were appealed to, new housewifely virtues
were developed, and a pathos of motherliness was in-
dulged in. Using the example of the Korean War and
the glaring breakdown of many soldiers, Betty
Friedan showed the consequences of overprotective
motherliness which, in this modern society with its
separation of the spheres of work and life, produces
only childish and irresponsible people. She demanded that, instead of sinking back into "animalistic
nature," woman should return to work, stand up for
herself in the professions, and leave the household
chores to someone hired to do so.

The Frenchwoman and the American both looked
down on the animalistic-corporal with the arrogant
glance of the intellectual woman. Both are oriented
toward male ideals which are removed from or
hostile to the body; and both start new education and
consciousness raising with criticism of woman's
alleged nature and natural duty.

Kate Millet—and her follower Alice Schwarzer—
made the most radical break with the previous concept of nature. They saw the subjugation of woman
in existing sexual practices. Not capitalism but
sexism—the subjugation of one sex by another—is
the real alienation of a human being. To them, then,

coitus is "the model of sexual politics on an individual or personal plane."[3] Their interest lies in exposing the power of the patriarchal system, which could develop on the basis of sexual domination. Kate Millet wrote:

> [This domination is] more rigorous than class stratification, more uniform, certainly more enduring. . . . Our society, like all other historical civilizations, is a patriarchy. . . . The military, industry, technology, universities, science, political office, and finance—in short, every avenue of power within the society, including the coercive force of the police—are entirely in male hands. . . . What lingers of supernatural authority, the Deity . . . ethics and values, the philosophy and art of our culture—its very civilization—is of male manufacture.[4]

Thus the mother always prepared to sacrifice herself, the secretary making coffee for her boss, the housewife always willing to serve, the underpaid female worker, all appear to be victims of and illustrations for sexual domination—illustrations of alleged female nature kept socially immature.

The age-old subjugation of women was discharged in a Gnostic freedom binge which first claimed to be hostile to the body and alien to nature, and then felt

3. Kate Millet, *Sexual Politics* (New York: Doubleday, 1970), p. 22.
4. Ibid., p. 25.

mockingly superior to everything irrational, cosmic, and mythical.

In her search for social maturity, woman has discarded the old nature and its rules of behavior as she would discard an outmoded dress. At the moment she is still indecisive, not knowing whether she should be more emotional or more rational. She must espouse militant rational methods in the present struggle for the freedom of her sex. Yet, besides her jeans, she also knows long skirts as an option. She is lonely, but independent. Marriage in its traditional form is a product of culture which demands self-denial. She is not prepared, "at the cost of suffocation," to oppose "the sinful world with the virtuous home."

The struggle for woman's social coming of age has shown that woman can no longer be put off with reproductive, complementary, and compensatory activities. Nor can she be explained on the basis of receptive, accepting, passive, open behavior patterns. She can be just as productive, creative, and active in leadership as man, and she can tackle matters just as rationally, actively, and persistently. But the struggle for social maturity also makes clear that the pushy male ideal includes a loss of wholeness. The behavior patterns contemptuously cast aside as "woman's nature" no longer have much currency in the new feminist movement. But the pressing question is:

what significance do they have for a more human life, for human beings and for society?

IV. THE BODY'S COMING OF AGE

Today, for the first time, a new human being stands out, one who is not exclusively oriented toward man and male ideals, who has a body of his/her own and a new sensitivity. It is not clear yet what he/she really is, what characteristics he/she possesses that are not shaped by education, society, or the expectation of other people. This is where fantasies and dreams begin, hopes for a new corporeality and sexuality that are no longer models for dominating and being dominated but rather models for new sensitivity and openness to the needs of the other. The search for the body's coming of age, however, has only just begun; and where at first it ended only with justification for and defense of lesbian love, it has remained unsatisfying.

But the search for new corporeality has still other dimensions. The feminist movement, begun by the Enlightenment, finds itself in the difficult position today of having cracks showing in the abstract, technical, and intellectual values and norms set by the Enlightenment. The limitations of growth are becoming clear for the first time in the history of mankind, as well as the catastrophic consequences of control and exploitation of nature and peoples, and of unrestrained economic expansion. In the private realm—especially in the schools—there are signs of sickness and doubts about our achievement-oriented society, and questions for new criteria and new happiness are cropping up.

The Enlightenment began with the discovery of reason and will as the marks of human character, and the movements for emancipation that built on this discovery altered the state, the economy, and society to accord with this image of humanity. But when, in the eighteenth century, one announced the primacy of will and reason, one forgot the human being's corporeality or, like Descartes, understood the body as a machine that was dominated, controlled, directed, and thus finally subjugated. Where one rediscovered corporeality, one peeled away from the emancipation movement, projected corporeality into woman's body, and understood woman as the model of passive nature and receptive corporeality. In this way the emancipation movements forgot and suppressed the corporeality of the human being; and wherever the idea was propagated, it led to a reactionary counter-movement such as in the Third Reich and the time of the American feminine mystique.

Even where today "sisterhood is powerful" is discovered and cared for, and where a new independent, self-conscious femininity and identity in society and history are searched for, there remains the question of whether the longing for a never-existing matriarchy is a fantasy with no reference to reality.

The dreams of a return to nature, of "another heaven and another earth," of pagan mother-goddesses who will unseat the patriarchal God and the man Jesus, at times seem like a Dionysian delirium after a pre-Enlightenment existence. But the question that should be put to today's feminist movement is: how can we reincorporate the forgotten corporeality into emancipation?

The corporeality conceived of as passive and controllable became clear to the age of the middle class in the image and model of woman. "The caring absorption in a world needing care" was, according to Buytendijk, the blueprint for woman's way of life. Out of this her existence developed in "permission." But her "total receptivity" was at the same time "lack of intentionality." The moral demand for selfless love, devotion, sacrifice was encountered in the idea of femininity as "the crown of nature." Thus female existence was always a "being-bodily-in-the-world." This is why housework could be seen as "woman's nature" and woman could be connected with climate and geography instead of history.

Simone de Beauvoir protested against this female receptive form of existence by positing the active form of existence, in which corporeality appears as, at most, directed corporeality (artificial insemination). For Shulamith Firestone, there is no longer any experience of special corporeality.

The autonomous "I" has suppressed its corporeality in the Enlightenment-binge and on the road to integration. But the realization today that a human being is not pure freedom allows us to discover the feeling aspect, the receptive, and the corporal—heretofore one-sidedly projected into woman—as forms of existence for both sexes.

On the social level, Herbert Marcuse saw the future of the feminist movement and the only realistic alternative to capitalism today in the exercising of receptivity: This, ". . . originating on the biological-social foundation, could bring about the realization of a new principle of reality, because [female qualities] represent the antitheses to the values held by the ruling capitalistic society." The radical feminist movement, which had started to attack Margaret Mead's characterization of woman as "constructive receptivity," was still reacting angrily to the "role of pacifism" which would thus be expected of it. But Existentialism, which considered the human being uninhibited, free, and self-supporting, has, in the course of time, become obsolete.

The only true human being is one who is willing to expose him/herself and be touched, be it by the world or by another human being. The "letting-oneself-go" of the mystics, body-building movements, contemplation and meditation are today pressing themselves on us again as human forms of living. The

image of humanity that still partly determines the
feminist movement—for example, the woman whose
autonomy has been betrayed by children, for whom
the husband fulfills the role of chemical substance—
needs to be revised.

To women and to the feminist movement, this
could mean that corporeality and physical experience
are no longer suppressed but accepted. In that case,
anatomy would not be fate any longer, it would be
opportunity. The question of how far the Pill can
represent the chemical directing of nature also
belongs here. Woman has an advantage over man in
her physical experience, "her greater capacity for
suffering and emotion" (H. E. Richter). This experience, applied to society, would no longer drive
her just into the house, into a female myth, or into a
feminine counter-movement; instead, it would allow
her to bring a new experience into a male-shaped
social world: self-exposure, allowing oneself to be
touched, and willingness to let the other person be.

But this can happen only if man becomes conscious
of his own body and its laws, and experiences corporeality anew. "If receptivity becomes a conscious
opening of oneself, if the feeling aspect becomes an
expressed willingness to let oneself be moved . . . if
care and motherliness rest on an expressed accep-
tance of the other in his otherness . . . then the
possibilities of the experience are no longer realizable

only within a passive lifestyle; then they are simultaneously placed between activity and passivity, between
doing and enduring" (Karen Böhme). For man this
would mean, for instance, to acknowledge and integrate dreams; not to suppress myths and images; to
bear disagreeable things; not to rationalize away conflicts; to include child-raising and housekeeping in
his life's plan; not just to relegate family planning to
his wife, but rather to offer himself to her "bodily";
and to practice all these things in his success- and
achievement-oriented life. Where this happens, man
can become more mature, woman can become more
free, and male-shaped society can become more
human. An ethic that includes feeling and a reason
that is libidinous could lead to new motivations for
human coexistence both in private and in society.

The vision of a complete human being was meant
to loosen the rational and aggressive phase of the
feminist movement. The Taizé brothers, with their
slogan "struggle and contemplate," could help their
sisters on their road to liberty. For women in the
Christian churches, this would mean experiencing
grace more totally, faith more corporally, and social
existence in greater solidarity with other women.

The struggle for intellectual and economic coming
of age was begun by men. The struggle for social
coming of age was carried on by minority groups and
women, and it ends today with the quest for corporal

coming of age. Women should be aware of their advantage; men should participate in this quest and this
struggle in order to attain their own suppressed and
forgotten corporal maturity. Only in this way can the
feminist movement become a humane movement to
all groups and to both sexes.

Woman between Self-Surrender and Self-Assertion

When I think of "self-surrender," I see before me the generation of my mother and grandmother: a very well-balanced, controlled, friendly, seemingly sane generation. When they were asked whether they would like another cup of coffee, they said, "But only if you are getting up anyway." And if one wanted to discover a wish or desire of theirs, they often responded, "Just whatever would suit you best. I'm always glad to go along."

In the next generation, self-surrender already expressed itself a bit differently: women who seemed very independent but who fell silent as soon as they were with their husbands, and with whom one talked for years about hundreds of unimportant matters. Sometimes they disclosed—mostly at a late and relaxed hour—what profession they had once wanted to enter, and what had filled them with enthusiasm and passion when they were young; a distinct personality then emerged from the anonymity of middle-class married life. Yet if one encountered them the next day, they had fallen back into anonymity and were once more devoted functionaries of married and family life.

And then there is the very young generation: one woman complains that she feels as though she were in solitary confinement since her second child was born and she no longer has career possibilities. When her small son asks her why she looks so sad, she answers quite frankly that she really doesn't feel like doing housework today and would much rather read.

Three generations: for the first, the role of self-surrender and adaptation has become like a dress or second nature. For the second, the self-fashioned and emphatically pleasant past is something like youthful foolishness, an early adventure one remembers almost with shame. Any conflict between desire and duty, being-oneself and marriage has long ago been buried and forgotten. And the youngest generation cultivates its emotions, its rights to its own identity; it expresses this conflict with fluency, objectifying it in economic or ideological terms.

What is "self-surrender" really? I would like to start, first of all, with the social conditions which have formed this concept. This is unusual to many people who live and think in the church; we are used to settling our problems in the realm of individual development, faith, and personal decision. But anyone who takes a sober look around has repeatedly experienced the power of external circumstances, the norms of the environment that shape us. Only if we include the realms of the alien and of dependencies in our calculations can we succeed in penetrating our own perplexity.

Self-surrender, self-sacrifice, is the undisputed, highest ethical norm of both state and church. Monuments are erected to the hero killed for his fatherland; Christ is honored for sacrificing his life for others. The cult of sacrifice is as old as humanity itself. It was present in pagan religions, and was incorporated into the Bible in modified form. Sacrifice makes human coexistence possible; sacrifice is what keeps humanity together. A sacrifice was made to Moloch so that the others could live in peace.

Modern Western industrial society is such a Moloch demanding the sacrifice of woman: women into the factories when industry needs them, if possible in the low-paying jobs; women as makeshift partners into all areas which have been weakened by technocratic society; women into the nursery when the birthrate has dropped; women into the home when the economy becomes paralyzed or when society either suppresses or relegates its sickness or inadequacy to the family. The thanks rendered to this victim are varied: the cult of Mary, the motherhood medal, Mother's Day. The ideology of motherhood

has eaten its way so deeply into society and our consciousness that it can at any time be brought into the
open when needed.

Added to these general social conditions which
have shaped the concept of "self-surrender" are,
secondly, the influences of our history, on which we
are dependent.

It seems to me that our German society is particularly prone to infection by the idea of woman's
self-surrender, and that we have much less inner
security or external antibodies to oppose it. (If we
meet women from other countries, we encounter
more self-confidence in their personal style and
public bearing.) Since the nineteenth century, we
have had a feminist movement whose leaders were
more interested in internal values and academic
education than in human rights or civil rights for
women. To them the word "Socialism"—meaning
change of political and social conditions—was an
apocalyptic bugbear. They had no contact with the
Socialist Women's movement, and consequently
never really shaped the general consciousness of all
classes.

At a time when, in other countries, the Enlightenment was celebrating its triumphs and some reflected
glory fell on women as liberated and equal beings
free to develop themselves, the war of liberation
against Napoleon started in Germany. The Enlightenment and human rights were discredited; sacrifice

for the fatherland became the model for humanity in the early nineteenth century, and women were given an "equal" share of it. Not the lady in the salon, not the suffragette fighting for human rights, but rather Louise—mother of many children and Prussia's queen in a time of need, who sacrificed her health, her life, and her pride to the fatherland—became the ideal of womanhood in Germany. The French expert on Germany, Robert Minder, justifiably pointed out that the German archetypes in culture and literature have been predominantly motherly types like Liselotte of the Palatinate, Goethe's mother, and Queen Louise. French literature, on the other hand, contained a large variety of female types—on the barricades, in the salon, and in the convent. Minder concluded that woman's role "is by definition modest in German literature."

The church deaconness—new symbol of devotion since the middle of the nineteenth century, the female parallel to the soldier in the wars of liberation—was the German contribution to the question of women's rights at the time. When the first women's colleges opened in the United States, our first deaconness houses were established. Ideas of woman's service, commitment, and sacrifice have repeatedly suffocated, or at least limited, all woman's autonomous endeavors. To be sure, these ideas did produce a broad spectrum of women's church work, stretching from the deaconness house through the diaconate

organization and parish aides to the German
Evangelical Women's League. But this work was
always encouraged by men (except for Amalie
Sieveking's solitary course) and always served to heal
the wounds of society rather than to change society;
it never had emancipation as a goal, and remained in
the ghetto of Christian or governmental ideas of
order. That is why the National-Socialist (Nazi)
glorification of biological motherhood met with
almost no serious resistance. Feminist movement and
equal rights were conceded to the unmarried, but to
this day there is a social taboo in Christian and conservative circles against liberation of the married
woman. And every Mother's Day the church re-
affirms—as does society, in the discussion on
paragraph #218 [a proposed change in German law to
allow abortion on demand]—that its ideal is still the
integrating, stabilizing, self-sacrificing mother rather
than the liberated and autonomous woman who has
created a personality of her own.

Today, woman's self-surrender does not even have
anything to do with "proud voluntary commitment"
to a cause. Self-surrender is a state one slides into
without having really chosen it. The nuclear family
has become the cause. Nest warmth or, as many people would say, the musty smell of such nuclear
families, clings to self-surrender, this highest ethical
norm. Whatever still had some dimension to it in the
age of agriculture and craftsmanship, whatever still

made some economic and moral sense in an extended family situation, has now shriveled to three or four people's egocentric alliance of interests. Prometheus has turned into Sisyphus, symbol of always-repeated and never-ending toil; courage and initiative are hardly ever required, surrender and flexibility always.

In the course of tolerant child-raising, much more reaction than action is expected; woman increasingly loses the ability to be "subject." Betty Friedan called this condition a regression to the animal level; if it is expressed positively and psychologically, it is called a stabilization of emotions. Woman's and mother's most beautiful task—expected by society and so often praised by the church—is, when seen in daylight, a daily guerrilla war unworthy of either the proud word "self-surrender" or its glorification. The family made famous in commercials (with a son and daughter, a place in the country, social security, desire for happiness, common freedom, preventive health and insurance against catastrophes and emergencies in life) seems to me, in the egocentricity with which it releases its members back into life, to be a distortion of the original meaning of self-surrender.

But let us leave the object that has become questionable and return to the subject itself. Let us assume there is a challenging project worth the commitment. Woman's self-surrender is demanded. But what is the self that woman is to surrender? I would

like to clarify the self of today's woman with the example of today's style of housing. In the last century,
there was the lady's drawing room, where she received visitors and where people assembled around
her. At the beginning of this century, in the very
masculine society of Wilhelm II, the man's study
replaced the middle-class drawing room. Today,
there is the all-leveling living room, and more em-
phasis is once again put on the children's room.
Children's rights have been discovered, the man's
working place has been set outside the home, but the
woman is permitted at most a desk next to the
dinette. The self of a woman in our culture is a self
without self-*consciousness,* without its own space. It
is a flexible and constantly readapting self, almost
never put to the test of deciding for itself. Adaptation
to the family's housing requirements, the children's
emotions, and the husband's working conditions and
working place conforms to demands of adaptation in
professional life: integration into a male society of
achievement, and assumption of preexisting male
behavior patterns. The image of being-without-self is
then crowned by that often praised female flexibility
which—as it is always put so well—will always
guarantee women a working place, in every situation
and in every form of society.

This "super-adapted" woman, adapted to family
and career, is the target of feminists' attacks. It is the
woman without a self of her own, not yet conscious

of *her own* capabilities, *her own* lifestyle, or *her own* needs; a convenient and useful member of a society in which—as psychotherapist Margaret Mitcherlich says—"successful narcissism" is almost impossible for a woman.

The older generation, due to its training, tended to consider its own self-realization a sin against God and society. The result was often a negation of personality which caused the female traits so frequently mocked: gossiping, female cunning, talkativeness, erratic behavior, subjectivity. The younger generation, despite all resistance, think they have realized a piece of their self. But is it really their own self, self body and soul, mind and reason, a self that is whole and undivided? Or isn't it rather once again a denial of what that self really is and should be?

Our self is torn, split between career and family, husband and children, duty and pleasure, adaptation and protest. We are asked to provide security and exercise our liberty, to fulfill the demands for a higher quality of life and bring forth achievements. We are the victims of guilt complexes, and we are often angry. We have an inkling of what our self could be: neither man's compensation nor a copy of him, but rather a development of all the values neglected in our society, such as tolerance, spontaneity, communication, and creativity. The split between our reality and the role-thinking taught to us is becoming more and more visible. We have long known the menopausal illnesses caused more by the loss of an inculcated role than by a change of hormones; more recent are the insights into the environmentally conditioned old-age depressions caused by a life emptied of meaning, lived without the challenge and security of the extended family. The increasing number of professional women suffering from stomach and heart troubles is well known; according to the latest statistics, the career woman dies five to six years before her husband, whereas the non-working woman outlives her husband by five to six years. We could comfort ourselves with the assurance we are getting, from many sides in West Germany, that man's emancipation is more necessary than woman's or we could be encouraged by H. E. Richter in his book *Lernziel Solidarität (Educational Goal: Solidarity),* with the statement that woman has an advantage in her liberation because of her greater capacity to suffer. But as long as social reality does not agree with these newly discovered values, they will remain only the first steps toward a new consciousness.

Where do we begin to search for our lost self? I would like to clarify this with two literary examples: Berthold Brecht and the Bible. In his calendar stories, Brecht told the story of the unworthy old woman: for years a woman raised her children and took care of her husband and the apprentices in his tradesman's shop. When the children left home, the husband died, and the business was dissolved, she started a new life at the age of seventy. She did things everyone considered "unworthy": she went to the movies, drank red wine, played cards, ate in restaurants—she, who had previously cooked for others and, most of the time, had eaten the leftovers. The attentions that her family had previously accepted as a matter of course she now lavished on a little crippled kitchen maid. She bought her a hat with red roses, invited her to her home, and took her out. A woman without self discovered another self after sixty years, a self characterized by joy, spontaneity, a new, free choice of people and relationships.

Another irritating literary figure is Mary in the Bible. While Martha, in conformity to her role as woman, hurries into the kitchen to prepare something nice for the guest, Mary, in violation of law and order, sits down at the feet of the teacher—a revolution against established custom. We long ago transformed this vexatious woman into the obedient, listening, receptive type of Christian woman, whereas, according to the witness of the New Testament, a revolutionary escape of women from law, custom, and tradition had resulted from Jesus' coming. Resurrection—the break through the structure of this existence—is often documented through and by women in the Bible. Two raisings from the dead occur for women; the third was a woman herself raised

from the dead. Even though established law forbade
women to be witnesses, it was women who were the
first witnesses to the resurrection!

Brecht's unworthy old woman and the Bible's
revolutionary Mary puncture society's imposed roles,
and obey a new law of freedom, passion, and spontaneity. Their opposites—the worthy old woman con-
tinuing to play her role, and the serving Martha—are
in no way condemned; they only withdraw into the
shadows. "The structure of living for others"
(Phyllis Chesler) withdraws in favor of a self-interest
seemingly egotistic, self-searching, self-loving, and
self-realizing.

How can we, with our conscience and with the expectations we and others have of us, cope with this
new role? Christian women will ask, "Then where is
love?"

There is a legend about a woman who was ordered
to jump over a stream, but who refused to do so
because she feared her love would be left behind.
When she finally did ford the stream, she found her
love on the other side. The search for the self begins
by freeing oneself from the attitude of sacrifice and
by opening oneself to one's own true spontaneity.
Willing sacrifice establishes no new relationships to
people; it renews nothing, it only creates new dependencies. Only when we have given up the sacrificial attitude do we experience a new emotional relationship
to people, things, and circumstances. Playing a role,

when it has become routine, demands only a part of one's self. A real, dedicated relationship demands the total person and bears within itself the promise of being true love.

The adventure of discovering oneself as a total human being signifies liberation and pain at the same time. Liberation, because it teaches us to discover stunted sides of our personality; because it allows us to experience anew the limitations and the totality of our physical, psychic, and mental unity; because it means rejecting excessive physical demands, psychically stabilizing top efficiency, or mental stress due to adaptation to a male-structured world. Liberation, because the pressures, which even the allegedly happy housewife is at the mercy of (all those comparative augmentations in achievement such as "better housing," "healthier eating," "better living") can be exposed. Such augmentations in achievement are not necessarily augmentation in the quality of life; for they promise so much happiness and can bring so much bondage.

But the adventure of discovering oneself also signifies pain because it uncovers fears, entanglements, and entrapment in roles and attitudes which one cannot resolve or which one is unwilling to resolve. It often signifies the recognition of waste and the reduction of many things; and it will frequently lead to loneliness and isolation. Our environment and our society will be repelled by this process of structural change, and will in no way be willing to honor it as long as it does not bear fruit that can be harvested. This creates guilt feelings, new dependencies, and conflicts one has never learned to overcome. To experience wholeness means to encounter society's limitations. How do we get out of this dilemma?

What we need today is *a strategy of self-assertion*. The word "self-assertion" makes theologians uneasy, for it reminds them of humanity's ungodly autocracy. It also reminds every set of parents of their child's obstinate phase, and every teacher of his student's necessary maturing process. For too long we have searched for woman's lost self in a partnership—as polarity, compensation, coordination, etc. Today's feminists justifiably warn us that such a "partnership" is the sleeping pill of emancipation. Woman's finding-herself is a process of self-assertion. It begins with a "yes" to herself, with an attempt to accept herself with her own desires, joys, and fears, a "yes" to a new "I" without ambition and without copying male style. But this process cannot then be concluded just privately with the marital partner; it must be released from our traditional internalizing, and it must lead to forms of self-assertion in society. Our own confusion, illness, and sin are also our society's confusion, illness, and sin, and therefore can be healed only in and with society.

Woman should discover herself as a whole human

being, but not stay stuck in a self-reflective "I" relationship. Rather, she should see herself as a member of a sick society in need of healing. Structures do not heal by themselves and are often immune to solitary fighters. The American women's liberation movement speaks of "pressure groups." I would prefer to consider them forms of self-assertion in our society; forms that are not ideals or ends in themselves, but that are necessary, helpful, and at some time dissoluble.

Some forms of self-assertion would be, for example: (1) small women's groups concerned with self-discovery and consciousness raising; (2) women's groups who press for emancipation in politics or church; (3) women's groups who, mindful of their own social oppression, work to liberate other oppressed minorities.

A woman's professional work does not necessarily have anything to do with self-assertion, although that is still often assumed. But perhaps self-assertion is unthinkable without some shred of public responsibility.

Dependencies and social conditions can be seen through more easily in these forms of self-assertion, and a consciousness of self can grow which more easily grasps the different dimensions of our existence. This is an area for experimentation in *new* partnerships (which are rumored to be particularly bad among women). Here other fringe groups can be better understood, because of one's own experience. The necessity for man's emancipation, for his liberation from the pressures of achievement and "masculinity," becomes visible. On the basis of new experiences, one can better test how one can take children more seriously while nevertheless letting them go. And there is the possibility of a *new sense of self-surrender* which no longer commits the split, adapted, or negated "I" into action, but instead has found itself and its tasks.

A precise description of the "I" would be science fiction, but certainly emotion and reason, objectivity and passion would no longer need to be opposites, and our Western separation of spirit and body would no longer be correct. Biologically, hormonally, men tend more toward aggressiveness, women more to empathy. The *model of an aggressive reason,* borne by women, could arise out of the existing scheme of a seemingly reasonable aggressiveness. This is a long-range view and there is a long way to go; but utopias are necessary to encourage the taking of first steps.

According to the words of our late President Gustav Heinemann, the church should march at the head of the revolution, not at the tail-end with the field kitchen. But church statements regarding problems of the day usually trail their development; these statements bless and confirm in retrospect what can no longer be changed or what has long ago become social reality. The causes for this are the church's long dependence on an absolute ruler, and the theological tradition of the so-called two kingdoms doctrine, out of which comes our broken relationship to public responsibility and our distrust of society. Our withdrawal from the world into the family and our uneasiness about letting our children be educated in all-day schools stem from this. Our secular society seems to have drifted away from ecclesiastical tutelage long ago, but a centuries-old consciousness training, carried on by church and society together, cannot be wiped out in one day.

In 1974 in Berlin, during the World Council of Churches Conference on Sexism, one experienced, however, a Christendom freeing itself from tradition and social entanglements. This Christendom was discovering its prophetic function of pointing to the future and being connected to society, and it really was marching at the head of a revolution to liberate humanity. Thus, for example, Mother's Day was critically examined, and another Day for Women was proposed which would more strongly emphasize their responsibility in the public sphere. Thus "partnership" was not understood as polar complementation on a private level, as it usually is in this country, but as a community of those who, despite their differences, recognize each other's rights and *both* make sacrifices. Partnership was removed from the concept of roles still prevalent among us, according to which one partner contributes a bit more sacrifice and warmth, and the other a bit more money and achievement. "Partnership" was removed from its narrow familiar frame and discovered in the most varied spheres of life and work. Thus women's liberation was seen in, with, and under the liberation and reordering of society.

It will take some time for these things to succeed in our church. It is even possible that ideas about women's public responsibility will again get mixed in with our traditional views of duty and service. Woman's task would then become a new self-surrender without self. There is already talk in the church about a three-phase theory, according to which woman, after completing her education and after her children are raised, would enter a third phase by again embarking on a career and public responsibility—without fully considering the presuppositions and consequences, the humiliations and disappointments connected with this, and without respecting the desires or pressures of young mothers to have careers. There is already talk of women "in service" and "on duty," and that is not far removed from the old diaconistic self-dissolution of women.

In a church which has preached—particularly to women—more Kant than Christ, one should begin with the joy of life, the "yes" to personality, the pleasure in wholeness and the courage to follow one's own road. An Englishwoman at the Conference on Sexism said, "It is wonderful to be a woman and a

Christian." Brecht said, about the unworthy old woman, "She had tasted the long years of servitude and the short years of freedom, and had consumed the bread of life down to the last crumb. . . . " That which has been called "the justification of the sinner" in traditional ecclesiastical language begins where one leaves the alleged security of one's private atmosphere, discards one's fears, and searches for the happiness and adventure of true self-realization. This can happen in a variety of forms: in a nuclear family which adopts children and becomes an open family, as well as in a political sphere. The promise is not one of success and recognition, but of experiencing large space, discovering undeveloped possibilities, and experiencing a new existence as woman and human being.

One will have to go on playing a part of the old role of "self-surrender"; one will make the painful discovery that "self-assertion" is not desired by society and church; and one will, above all, be lonely. But one will increase one's awareness of those who have lost their freedom, and of oppressive structures. And one will no longer slip into this *newly* possible self-surrender submissively, unwillingly, or with Christian matter-of-factness. It will be a self-surrender which, in the joy of its own newly won freedom, has no choice but to translate this freedom into action.

Theses Regarding the Emancipation of Women in Church and Society

1. More Kant than Christ has been preached to women in the church. In many Christian circles, self-surrender is to this day considered duty, while self-realization and self-love are considered sin. Our "yes" to our "I" should begin with the fact that God's love makes us lovable even in our own eyes.

2. Real self-surrender can only occur where there is a self to surrender. In our society and our church, the self of a woman is an adapting, stopgap, and assisting self; this self has no space, function, or consciousness of its own.

3. Today's women need a strategy of self-assertion to find their lost self. Self-discovery cannot be accomplished solely in the private or personal realm. Self-discovery must also occur in forms of self-assertion, in all kinds of women's groups in which economic and psychological dependencies are disclosed and new forms of coexistence are tested.

4. Partnership can be the sleeping pill of emancipation. Only the person who is alone can also be one of a twosome; only the person who is whole can give totally.

5. Woman is not just the complementary opposite of man; she is a fully independent personality neither subordinated to man (Luther to Bonhoeffer), nor coordinated with him (Karl Barth). The biological differences are of much less and the sociological differences (e.g., education) of much greater importance to the shaping of the sexes than was earlier thought. What a woman really is, what kind of *true* partner to man she can be, will only be seen when the role-expectations for both sexes are decreased.

6. Motherhood is a limited biological phase for a woman, which necessitates particular attitudes, such as support. But these attitudes are not lifelong definitions of woman's nature. Churches and conservative societies cultivating such a cult of motherhood obstruct women's full creative development of their personality.

7. According to Gal. 3:28, the old order of creation (Gen. 1:27) was repealed in Christ. In view of the coming kingdom of God, therefore, there are no longer any differences between peoples, classes, and sexes in the church. We must not be satisfied with the claim that this only applies "before God *(Coram*

Deo)" and has no social reality. The church should be pioneering a new social position for women.

8. Diaconate and emancipation need not be opposites. But, in our Christian tradition, diaconate was for too long and too one-sidedly considered healing of society's wounds, without regard for the number of wounds society itself inflicted. Today, the need is seen for a "structure-altering diaconate" alongside this "diaconate in structures." Women's diaconate, therefore, is not an obsolete phase but, in this expanded understanding of diaconate, a challenge to the woman come-of-age and critical of society.

9. Many aspects of Western technocratic achievement-oriented society are being questioned today. The limits of growth have been reached, but we are still determined in the public, educational, and private realms by an expansionist ethic of achievement. Women possessing new self-consciousness and new feelings of self-worth could establish new standards of tolerance, communication, creativity, spontaneity, etc. in this area.

10. Man's emancipation is not identical with woman's emancipation. One should not confuse the two, since they start with different presuppositions. However, a woman who is aware of her own oppression and her possible liberation will simultaneously have increased awareness of man's bondage and the

oppression of fringe groups in our society. Her own freedom will always be a commitment to the freedom of others.

Bibliography

WOMAN IN THE NEW TESTAMENT

Bachofen, J. J. *Das Mutterecht*. Frankfurt, 1975.

Borneman, Ernest. *Das Patriarchat*. Frankfurt, 1975.

Brooten, B. "Junia . . . Outstanding among the Apostles." Manuscript, Tübingen, 1976.

Brown, R. E. "Women in the Fourth Gospel." *Theological Studies* 36, no. 4., Baltimore, 1975.

Cancik, Hubert. "Die neutestamentlichen Aussagen über Geschlecht, Ehe, Frau." *Zum Thema Frau in Kirche und Gesellschaft*. Stuttgart, 1972.

Gaiser, Konrad. *Hausregeln für das Leben von Mann und Frau im Späthellenismus*. Tübingen, 1975.

Kähler, Else. *Die Frau in den paulinischen Briefen*. Zurich, Frankfurt, 1960.

Parvey, Constance F. "The Theology and Leadership of Women in the New Testament." *Religion and Sexism*. New York, 1973.

Schüssler-Fiorenza, Elisabeth. *Der vergessene Partner*. Dusseldorf, 1964.

———"Die Rolle der Frau in der Urchristlichen Bewegung." *Concilium* 12, no. 1 (1976).

Stendahl, Krister. "Die biblische Auffassung von Mann und Frau." *Menschenrechte fur die Frau.* Munich, 1974.

Thraede, Klaus. "Art. Frau." *RE* (1970).

Wolff, Hanna. *Jesus der Mann.* Stuttgart, 1975.

FOUR STATIONS ON THE ROAD TO
WOMAN'S COMING OF AGE

Beauvoir, Simone de. *Das andere Geschlecht.* Hamburg, 1960. *The Second Sex.* Translated from the French by H. M. Parshley. New York, 1949.

Bebel, August. *Die Frau und der Socialismus.* Berlin, 1964.

Böhme, Karen. *Zum Selbstverstandnis der Frau.* Meisenheim, 1973.

Braun, Lily. *Memoiren einer Sozialisten.* Berlin, undated.

Buytendijk, Frederick Jacobus. *Die Frau.* Köln, 1953. *Woman: A Contemporary View.* Translated from the German by Denis J. Barrett. Glen Rock, 1968.

Chartschew, A. G., and Golod, S. J. *Berufstätige Frau und Familie.* Berlin, 1972.

Chesler, Phyllis. *Frauen, das Verruckte Geschlecht.* Reinbeck, 1974.

Dernemann, Luise. *Clara Zetkin.* Berlin, 1973.

Firestone, Shulamith. *The Dialectics of Sex.* New York, 1971.

Friedan, Betty. *Der Weiblichkeitswahn.* Hamburg,

1966. Translation of *The Feminine Mystique.* New York, 1963.

Hoppe, Else. *Gestalt und Liebe.* Hamburg, 1934.

Lange, Helen. *Lebenserinnerungen.* Berlin, 1922.

Kant, Immanuel. *Was Ist Aufklärung?* Göttingen, 1967.

Marcuse, Herbert. "Marxismus und Feminismus." *Jahrbuch Politik,* vol. 6, no. 7.

Mead, Margaret. *Mann und Weib.* Hamburg, 1958. Translation of *Male and Female, a Study of the Sexes in a Changing World.* New York, 1949.

Millet, Kate. *Sexus und Herrschaft.* Munich, 1971. Translation of *Sexual Politics.* New York, 1970.

Moltmann-Wendel, Elisabeth, ed. *Menschenrechte fur die Frau.* Munich, 1974.

Richter, Horst Eberhard. *Lernziel Solidaritat.* Reinbeck, 1974.

Schmidt, Alfred. *Der Begriff der Natur in der Lehre von Karl Marx.* Frankfurt, 1962. *The Concept of Nature in Marx.* Translated from the German by B. Fowkes. London, 1971.

Schwarzer, Alice. *Frauenarbeit—Frauenbefreiung.* Frankfurt, 1973.

Stefan, Verena. *Häutungen.* Munich, 1975.